Longing for Latitude

Longing for Latitude

poetry by
Alan C. Howard

Greenroom Press • 1998

Library of Congress Card Catalog Number: 97-94737
ISBN 0-9661463-0-1
Manufactured in the United States of America

"Daughter" was originally published in *The Free-Floating Mind*. "Ignis Fatuus," "At the Sleeping Bear Dunes," and "Vectors" were first published in *Passages North*. "Gletsch Pass, Switzerland," "Roots," "The Abscission Layer," and "In Some Distant Land" originally appeared in *Serendipity*. "Sic Transit" was originally published in *Caprice*. "Christmas" and "Zen Haiku" first appeared in *Poet's Fantasy*. "Hiroshima" was originally published in *Echoes*. "How to Become a Poet" was first published in *Feh!*. "The Children of Malawi" was originally published in *Oracle*.

Cover photograph by Lorenz/Avelar.

For Judy, my most auspicious discovery.
For Jennifer and Rebecca, my most poetic creations.

And for the three teachers who lit the lamp
of creative writing for me:
Mrs. Wynn Bade, Traverse City High School
Dr. Clifford Josephson, San Francisco State College
Dr. William Butt, Central Michigan University
I'm sorry these words of gratitude
have come too late.

Contents

Yamamoto tea:
Evening with the Buddha,
Nirvana's foretaste.

Images of Life

the guru speaks:
life is, among other things,
a quick kiss between eternities,
shorter than a snow angel's memory;
a flicker in the candle of parenthood;
a photo album overflowing with
the strangers we have become;
memory whitewashed with desire;
smiles, some real; obligations forgot;
breakdowns, automotive and nervous;
volcano of puberty, cough of old age;
an opportunity to bury six dogs.

and, if that's not enough, it is
a basement full of hammers and rasps
and *national geographic* dreams;
several divorces and a marriage or two;
destruction of buildings that inhabit us;
laughter of regret; electric filament health;
alphas, omegas, birth on cold steel;
final good-byes over astroturf;
necessity, calamity, frivolity;
raison d'être for earth and its gods;
something to do between cigarettes.

Vectors

These dreams of mine choke on themselves,
Stalling in their upward flight
While I curse them for their birth,
These bastard mementoes of a time
When the wind didn't blow my hair away.
Yet I hoard them like Christmas fudge,
A hedge against that December day
When some legitimate child of mine
Will fly into my room on wings
Of something I forgot, and deftly ask me
Why I live.

Wounded Knee, South Dakota

High on the hill,
Overlooking the mass grave,
A young Sioux warrior
(A man whom dreams forgot)
Sells dreamcatchers to tourists
Who collect massacres
To hang on den walls.
For them the brisk, forgiving wind
Erodes a century of shame.

But in Pine Ridge
At Taco John's takeout
The teenage servers know
That Big Foot dies a little
With every enchilada they sell.

Just the same, not far from here
The bones of Crazy Horse
Ennoble the grateful earth.
Some fine spring day
They will sprout a phoenix flower
Around which the ghost dancers
Will move in supplication,
Awaiting the red messiah
That won't be bought or sold.

Stopping at a Roadhouse in Ebenezer in the Northern Territory (for Judy)

Outside, the lightning strikes,
A fierce flash of big-bang bravado,
And then, as the planet spins,
The low, leonine rumble comes,
Frightening the camels and the kangaroos
That huddle under the dead gum trees.

Inside, between the flicker of incandescent lights,
The stockmen mumble in their billy tea:
"First desert rine in three months," they say,
As we sidle up to our own table,
Free for now from a coachload of tourists
From Altoona and Peoria, hayseeds like us.

Our repast is ready—jam, fluffy cream,
Your first scones, my millionth cigarette—
While in the gift shop a hundred didgeredoos
Whisper ditties to deaf Caucasian ears,
Songs heard by none but a few native gods
Hanging in the damp rafters.

Down on the floor a ghost appears,
An aborigine, apparition in my smoke,
Trailing a wake of yesterdays,
His long-ago eyes reflecting the Dreamtime,
The racial creation before his personal birth.

And, looking at him through modern spectacles,
Absorbing the ages that have fashioned him anew,
I think today is our dreamtime, yours and mine,
The ancient, seasonal renewal of our love.

As spirits burst through the dark red earth,
Soaking dry roots with the warm winter rain,
Spawning carpets of spinifex for the kookaburra,
We rise anew on this far, old continent,
Energized by thunder and warm tea,
Reborn like this year's outback weeds,
Closer than this dense, humid, electric air,
Secure as a joey in a marsupial's pouch.

Forest, my *zendo*.
Young chipmunk, my Zen master.
Man without *sangha*.

Sic Transit

Here in Madrid my father and I are
Playing hooky from the school of life,
Sleeping late, reeking of garlic,
Admiring *The Naked Maja* in the Prado,
Smoking Cuban cigars in Retiro Park,
Sipping sangria in the Plaza Mayor.

Forty years ago my father walked me home
From kindergarten in a December blizzard.
Today, in this sultry July afternoon,
I direct my lost father to the hotel
And remind him to carry his keys.

Tonight we'll dine at Botin's,
Papa Hemingway's favorite refuge.
I'd like to say that we'll discuss our
Next forty years, but I know we won't.
Instead, we'll chat about old times,
Enjoy the succulent suckling pig,
And share one more pitcher of that
Sweet, sweet, sweet sangria before
The waiter blows out the candle.

Sailing to Paris

Sometimes, when the wind
From the past wafts memory
With the spring's scents of desire,
I like to sing aubades
To decay, our Siamese twin,
And take out a lease on 1972.
So Nixon's my landlord.
I don't care.

I'll return to Paris,
My bell-bottom Byzantium,
And commandeer a seat
At a sidewalk cafe
On the Champs Elysees.
Free at last,
I'll chain-smoke Gaulois,
Drink a Stella Artois for every
Good idea I've ever had,
And admire the young women
With granny glasses,
Ironed hair, and tie-dyed minds.

I will not have heard of AIDS,
Or cholesterol, or common sense,
Nor anticipate the paralysis of divorce,
Or the death of those I thought immortal.
Instead, I'll lift a glass to youth,
That beautiful, stupid chanteuse
Who sleeps in every morning
Because there will always be
Another dawn.

Crossing the Equator

Night flight three, London to Lusaka.
I choose a window seat, settle into myself.
We lift off late, soar over the Channel,
Then the invisible chateaux of the Loire,
And then there is no light except for
The luminous crescent of Marseilles and
The full moon I brought from Michigan.
Over the Sahara we penetrate a vast
Blackness not dreamt of in my philosophy.
Captain Mwanda comes on, coughs,
Says we're crossing the Equator over Zaire.

Somewhere down there Marlow pursues Kurtz,
Hearing a jungle rhythm more primeval,
More basic, than my rapid pulse.
My heart of darkness is down there, too,
A colossal globe that sucks tragedy
Out of the unwilling sky and into
The crocodile-swimming Congo basin.

Yet, tonight, I won't let that happen.
The alluring southern moon
Pulls my tides in directions that
No cartographer could ever measure.
Some people spend their lives
Searching for their other hemisphere.
Not this man—I'm going home
To an ocean full of brilliant stars
That half my world has never seen.
Make way for me, brave new half-world.
I'm flying into the arms
Of the Southern Cross.

Gletsch Pass, Switzerland

An Einstein
In these parts
Would understand:
Subtraction is the key
To know. To cross at night,
We bid the light farewell, and
Rise and lower gears with height.
One by one they angle out of life:
The tiny tumult of Brienz, and hope,
The taller trees and confidence, then
Streams and shrubs, till at the last zag,
We reach storm's eye and find what's left:
Our love, some snow, two liters of combustion,
A sky of earthbound tales, and, now that man
Is gone, man. Coming down we add—a hotel
On a precipice, a hiker on a windward
High, the tinny cow bells' clangs,
And, last, our camping place and
Radio Luxembourg. At rest we
Find—addition is the key to
Know. An Einstein in
These parts would
Understand.

The Sexton's Apprentice

Back when I was a very little boy,
I amused the earth with my sexton's spade,
Delving the loam to make homes for the overlooked:
Chipmunks, fish, a squirrel that met a wheel.
All these I consecrated for some animal heaven,
Topping them off with an orange-crate cross,
While, high in the loft of the neighbor's barn,
The girls of my class wrapped their plastic dolls,
Wearing motherhood like hospital gowns.
We all labored as we knew.
Only later, when I committed my dear one
To this indifferent planet for everlasting care,
And I saw the neighbor women
Pushing their prams past the graveyard gate,
Only then did I know, O sweet little girls,
That you never had anything on me.

Minnesota loon
Echoing in the far lake:
Moment of good karma.

At the Sleeping Bear Dunes

No skyborne seagull can beguile
A lofted thought from me, or call,
Like cherubs in some canvas oil,
My soul to disembodied joys.
No fishing in the sky for me.

Instead these acres I'll embrace
Of glacial sand that ran, and runs,
One inch a year to drown, someday,
The lake beyond with crystals from
This hibernating age.
I like my progress slow.

Grind eons in my mortar, gods,
Drop anchors in these shifting ribs,
Where western winds whip traceless wisps,
Upon a formless, normal face.
The skin can change, the rest endure.

Just sleep me with the sleeping bear;
Sing eras to my ears.
Tonight I'll hug the earth, and wake,
Gods willing, from an epoch's dreams,
Here, high atop this airy beach,
Where gulls ignore a grounded man.

Oceanic

A sudden burst of cloud begets
A camaraderie of cigarettes
Under the eaves of university,
Where weather talk and whether talk
Dry up my anomie.
A cycling someone asks her way
To somewhere that I never knew,
But with a smile. Meanwhile,
Our sons and daughters take their test,
While we, the elders, wait, all wet,
In competition's fellowship.
This spring, this chrysalis of years, presents
Our talk, a blackish bird with epaulets,
That flower that I never named but will.
And still the rain shall fall,
And I won't mind.
O world, I'm coming back to you.

Christmas

on after-autumn afternoons
when the sun hunkers low
on the cold southern line
and the winds foreclose
on the pith of your bones
you might forget that
love gave itself to you
to keep through the freeze
you might not remember
that druids wept over stones
for the memory of leaves
and you might not be astonished
when you recall
that saturnalian revelers
and frost-exhausted romans
stopped their retching
and excessing
just long enough to hear
the gods had a fire
we wouldn't have
to steal

At the Butterfly Sanctuary in Kuranda

under this dome
in the lush rain forest
some butterflies
live such short lives
that they are born
without mouths
before we leave australia
they will mate and die

on the flight home
my adult daughters
jennifer and rebecca
will cross my mind
then it will be time
for nature's bonus

once we lift off
I will sip coffee
enjoy rubber chicken
listen to rossini
touch my wife's hand
read kazuo ishiguro
watch *shadowlands*
chat with the young bloke
from new zealand
and gaze out the window
to find the equator
longing to see the line
that does exist
but isn't there

Daughter

Day darks, night brights, my mind thinking indrinks
    you in your crib justsleeping, breathing sighly,
    undriven dreaming, and I clockstuck grasp refracting
    rainbowed mindbeams of your justbornness,
    and I brainstrobe laughcries.

My brainstrobe timeprobes, kaleidostops,
    lasers my brightnow, rightnow flashes as I
    reeling touch you feeling my alwaysness—the
    of-my-self Eastermornborn newdawn no!-denial smile of
    you in your crib justsleeping—slidelike stillframed,
    sealedbeamed and everyhued.

But brainbeams also black refract, and I,
    forwardfilming, shuttershudder the toofastflicker,
    dreading and stalling the cradle-and-all downfalling
    and farewelling the nowmine mindpeace of
    you in your crib justsleeping, while I shun
    the gray, dark, dun someday youknow of myworld,
    insecuring and fearing your howcomes,
    and my dontknows.

Dontknows die though, unthings unseen unsought
    by the reflecting spectral under-ultra, over-infra
    pastel prism of birthshine, and I breathe
    an aura of aurora's child—
    you in your crib justsleeping—dawndreaming in your
        liferise,
    swaddled in tomorrowness, the echo of futurity
    and voice of starlight.

A Recently Divorced Man Visits Disney World

Like holograms in the Haunted Mansion
These ghostly families hover before me:
Moms, dads, daughters, sons,
Trailing balloons, wearing silly hats,
Dribbling ice cream on Goofy shirts.
They're so happy, my envy swells
With the helium above their heads.

Night, my only companion, sits beside me
Outside the Kitchen Pantry in the Village,
Where I munch cookies baked by strangers.
More families filter through the leafless trees,
Laughing, ignoring this odd, old bachelor,
While white lights blink at my loneliness.
Between the children's squeals Jiminy Cricket,
A disembodied fountain of purest joy,
Sings "When You Wish upon a Star."

My wishing stars, I think, are black holes,
Hoped-out embers sealed by legal decrees.
Even so, a man can stir his coffee with memory.
Ahead of me once stood a red caboose,
Where, in a happy spring, my children played.
Now it is gone, just as they are,
And February tells me to bundle up
My body and my thoughts of times past.

Yet, forty years ago, in *Cinderella*,
In *Lady and the Tramp*, in *Sleeping Beauty*,
Walt promised the child in me

That marital love would always endure,
That sparrows sing over everlasting rainbows.
But now I'm caught in a new-age parent trap.
A sense of failure dogs me like Pluto,
Nipping at the cuffs of my self-esteem.
I wear self-pity like old clothes.

"It's a Small World After All."
A new song seeps between the trees.
It's a small world, all right,
But sometimes I feel like an alien in it,
As obsolete as the skinny necktie I wear.
And how old is too old to start over?

But that's enough of that. Come morning,
I will take the shuttle to Tomorrowland,
Find a bench by Space Mountain,
Drink lemonade under a palm tree,
Throw away my tie, and watch the children
Of the new small world
As they wish upon their starships.

Tawny impala,
Grazing still on the high *veld*:
Joy of not killing.

On Learning of the Discovery Of Four-Million-Year-old Human Bones In Ethiopia

When my dog wags her tail
She's saying *carpe diem*
Like a lustful Renaissance poet.
She should know better.
We don't have a day to seize.
Two hundred thousand human generations
Have married the receptive earth.
In our cradles we learn to say goodbye.
On a night like this you might say
I drink nihilism with my cappuccino.
But no matter; on a crisp fall day
I enjoy a fine Mexican cigar,
And I recently noticed that your eyes
Are bluer than the Zambezi River
At Victoria Falls.

Roots

If my hair didn't grow
How would I know the trees
Or the breezes that bend them
Toward what a clock can record?
How would I know that love
Springs up as the air recedes,
The dead part first and then
The onion bulb that we weep from?

There is no telling what can be told,
And we're born too late for knowing.
The underpart that understands
Will rise as we die from our birth,
Taking our deathdays one by one
And trolling that line, that strand,
Inch by grudging inch.

Rainbow Prayer, Linkoping, Sweden, 1983

If the child is father to the man
And I am, God, too many men,
Then may this brilliant broken arc
Resolve itself into my natal day,
Deprismatize the bulb of my first,
My only, illumination.

Then let me grow anew,
A whiter light of untried possibility.
Let me incorporate, amalgamate, and integrate
The cross of the flag at this cross of my life,
The blue of the sky, the gold of the grain,
The verdancy of the grass when young
And the crimson blood
Of a still-responding heart.

But don't reduce me to a single beam.
Recreate me, a fascis of hues,
Polarize me and propel me straight,
That I may leave this neutral land
A partisan to a newer truth,
A heliotrope who finds his sun
Even in the night of the ominous,
Menacing storm beyond.

Slides of Dachau: A Dramatic Monologue (A German-American Remembers)

Well, here we are at Dachau now,
Enjoying our tailgate lunch
Over by the barbed wire there,
The day my hangnail hurt.
Never thought we'd be hungry
So soon after Heidelberg,
But you know what they say
About the wurst. We all
Must eat for *Lebensraum*.
Of course, I still feel bad about
Those poor folk who perished
So close to the Hofbrauhaus,
But then, didn't I get
A great shot of the barbecue pit
With my eff two point eight?
And wasn't it a swell summer?
But then, sometimes,
On winter nights like this,
When sleet wind blows against our panes,
And blazes flame in the Franklin stove,
And roaring coals bewarm the dog,
The slides will sometimes pass too fast
For time or Agfachrome to catch.
And when the beer and remote control
Can clarify our concentration some,
And show upon the lighted screen
The plastic trappings of our tourists' life,

The popcorn sticks with extra ease,
Attacking tacky hands and sleeves,
Rolling, rolling down our unarmed arms,
Glazing Aryan wrists and elbows with
A film of grease that,
Even in a thousand years,
Will never, ever wash.

An Extremely Hot Day in the Luxembourg Gardens

In the Luxembourg Gardens
Death has no sting, nor does it hum
A triad of resentment, sadness, or regret.
Instead, the victory sings in a hell transformed:
Leaves of chestnut over our heads,
Blossoms of plane in the blaze of the avenue,
Banish the wraiths with a sheltering shade,
Belie the torrid with something Hades hates,
Turning beer into nectar, cola into wine,
While, in the sun, the mower wrests submission
From eternal forces bent on city life.
Meanwhile, down the *rue* to which no sorrow
    clings,
Through the sweet, harmonious cacophony,
Dissonant chords of Citreön horns,
Mirage beams of a Pantheon alive,
Shimmer over the Boulevard Saint Michel,
Igniting conflagrations of geraniums,
Amid azaleas and the portable orange,
Into a scene that the sunburned eye,
As well as the grateful heart, can love.
Motion, heat, sweat, and thirst,
Transplanted Pans and palms alike,
Statuary in the dark and light,
Celebrate a moment wrenched from death,
A missed connection with the beckoning Styx,
Here, beyond the limbo of the lost,
In the *arrondissement* of the yet alive.

Hiroshima

On my way to Peace Memorial in Peace Park
I stop at the Peace Bridge on Peace Avenue.
The river, radioactive when my life dawned,
Flows too gently for one of my ancestral *angst*.
It sluices the gates of my culpability.

Then a flock of schoolgirls approaches.
Their giggles are more delicate
Than the imagined songs of origami cranes.
"*Konichiwa, gaijin*," they tweet,
Flashing three-kiloton smiles.
Their fingers peek from blue uniforms,
Making the peace sign, a fork to stab
The unintended target of my heart.

"Little girls," I say, in a language of eyes,
"This guilt of mine has no half-life."
Surprised, they only laugh,
Their voices a twitter of chirps,
And then, with guileless grins,
They fly away to an aerie atop Mount Fuji,
High above this dreadful world.

Blazing red sunrise,
Spinifex in the outback.
Oh, tranquility.

Circular Quay: Sydney: Noon

Sometimes it pays to feel antipodal.
Home harbors the heart, of course,
But a spherical lake of molten fire
Divides me from my town, my job,
The iron yoke of expectation.
Here, on this quay, I am closer
To the Sea of Tranquillity,
Free of the gravity that makes
A fixed address of my soul.
It isn't anomie; it's a fine sense of hydroponics,
A drawing of sustenance from the rarefied brine
That flows from Antarctica to a spot of time
Under the Coat Hanger Bridge.
The cobalt sky, the waves, the gulls,
These green-and-creme ferries to anonymity
Beckon me to become a citizen of impermanence,
Each jetty a finger pointing to a denial of destiny.
The Opera House, sails always erect,
Offers to transport me, but I resist itineraries.
Give me a perpetual passport,
>   One upside-down sun,
>   One true wife,
>   A bottomless pocket of travellers' cheques,
>   And I will happily dwell
>   In the lee of any prevailing wind.

Beyond the Veil

The only thing wrong with these
Less evanescent and increasingly more
Morbid intimations of mortality
Is that I know exactly, precisely,
Inevitably, inexorably, indubitably,
How I will spend January 6, 2102.

Unless I hang in a biology lab,
Clacking bicuspids on command,
A toy for tomorrow's tittering teens,
Or stuff a spittoon that could
Be put to better use,
I'll wake to a breakfast of frost.

Then, and probably before,
I'll weary of satin, miss my shoes,
Regret the pillow the mortician swiped.
Most of all, I will hate
To wear a tie on Saturday.

And then, there is an outside chance,
That I'll stare upward in a dream of brass,
Hoping that, before the rains erode my name,
I'll feel one twinge of what I know now,
Holding this silver pen in a pink hand
That spends every diurnal moment,
Each second, month, and day,
Squeezing harder than it did before.

The Abscission Layer

isn't it funny how
nature invites you over
welcomes your face
turns water to wine
gets you drunk
lays out linen
breaks out the silver
and the china cups
fixes coq au vin
or surf and turf
if you prefer
sings to you
lights your cigar
warms your toes
by the coals
and then
after the
star-spangled banner
escorts you to the door
opens it to
the sleety gale
and hugs you with
desperate love
right up to the
moment she kicks
you

out

Springtime Loves Detroit

springtime loves detroit
        more than it adores a place
where beauty and truth shake hands

down at the rouge plant,
        winter-dark and dingier
than the porno shops on woodward avenue,
                rivulets of rust
        wash acres of disappointment
                and snowbanks dwindle
                under a soot-veiled sun,
the city apollo of cadavered humankind

in cadillac square
        one crocus will sing alive
        and mend the spirit of a mendicant,
an aria that cadillac himself ignored
        when it was whispered
over an ocean of pine

and up the corridor
in dismal chicken shacks
and crack house lairs
of aging pimps and whores
        we find the urban renewal
that the hardest pavements can't retard—
the way a single blade of grass
        can sever despair,
birth and rebirth
bringing in their wake
the greatest force on earth

but the real renaissance center
is a puddle of mud in highland park,
        where the dead-ended homeboys—
        exhausted, lost, and blind to hope—
crack a skin of ice to find
the endless sea below

Dark blue Ulysses,
Impermanent butterfly:
Whom shall we become?

Ignis Fatuus

That asinine, deanimated X-rayed film,
A radiologist's cartoon of this, my once
And future skull, shall never spark
My photon-photoed brain to pray, or sigh, or cry
Alas or guzzle booze beyond a poet's or a jester's
Normal glut. It's just a joke.
A pumpkin head for every time and mood,
This foolish, phosphorescent jack o'lantern
Woos away my obligated sense of dread.
Instead, with moron grin and swamp gas glow
He mocks my woe's capacity. His head
Invites a glance, a laugh, a moment of autumnal
Mirth, a silly walk down membrane lane:
A trick-or-treat for introspective spooks.

Behold this filigree of cobwebs, cracks, and balls
Of luminescent dust that ages hence may well delay
The progress of a subway or a sewer pipe.
His flaws and flows unhid by hair or nose
Or noticeable skin, the apparition casts
A disrespectful dimestore leer to disinter
A prehistoric child's fright. He need not hold
His breath. Buffoons embody cheer, not moldy
Death and mutability. But yet, and then again,
When unilluminated by a candle's warmth, this
Sallow Play-Doh goblin of my dome-to-be emits
A silver nitrate sheen unseen by eyes eclipsed
In darkened orbits where I find no flame,
No wax, no wicks or wicked tricks, no upset
Garbage cans or dirty words on window panes,

No conflagrations on a porch nor torch to fire
A later blaze of autumn leaves, no breeze, in fact
No air at all and thus no windmills for a tilting
Brain to charge.   No pumpkin seeds.

Beneath a gangled forehead mess of veins, above
A solid lode of dental gold, there glows no flare
Of what I was, or am, or would become, no phantom
Symbols to exalt significance.   In darkened cells
Where still I store a hoard of calendars, a birthday
Cake or two, a catalogue of kindness, each and every
Compliment, a something meant for me alone, a stone
Set in a ring, a ball of disconnected strings,
Two tickets to a play, a game, a name, a prize,
A gag or two, degrees from schools, certificates of birth
And worth, I hear a vacuous wind through holes for ears
Long gone.   Without my triumphs and my comic lines
My head lies vanquished on a silvered plate,
My favorite parts by Roentgen's rays x'ed out.

Alas, poor fool, an antedated glass-electric ghoul
Has yoricked you before your time and galvanized you
With a joyless instant foreplay of your certain doom.
With negatives of light and time a mirrored pantomime
Of gloom reflects the specter of your jests and forces
Grizzly glimpses of your tailored destiny.   For this
Alone he suits you well.   Meet Jack the Shade,
A constant wise guy's constant friend.   From time to time
While you have time, this obverse watchman of your swamp's
Dark night will hallow with his hollow gallowed look
The sacred radiation of your laughing blood.
His pallor proves your frosted pulse; his shadowgraph

Restores the fulcrum of your wit. Now look into the glass:
The quick and silvered side is you. And from beyond the
Pale of sight the ancient face bespeaks a fitting cross of flame:
A customized memento mori for a melancholy modern clown.

The Children of Malawi

they're so aggressive, so imploring,
        the children of malawi beg for tambala
as if these coins could buy back the time
            before they became sick.

        as they supplicate they shake,
their rickety legs buckling under
           the imperial backpacks
        that they carry to school.
           though i play deaf
their open sores say "i accuse."

not so long ago
        the british viceroys shipped home
           ivory and responsibility
        in steamer trunks.
        they left behind
baskets of gin-and-tonic dreams
        that no one could lift.

when these children die,
        and it will be soon,
i'm going to lather all my tambala,
purchase the embers of their bones,
and scatter the sparks
        over the dry forests
           of the white man's mind.

Moguls

He who wakes in the morning
Deserves the *Croix de Guerre*.
Pouring coffee calls for applause,
Or a pause at least for prayer.

When you ski,
Just one second
Of one minute
Of one degree off parallel
Means that someday your tips
Will arrive in two different states.
Then you'll become a wishbone
Without a wish.

O God, dear God,
Dear punctured, gored,
And quarter-nailed Lord,
Don't let me be halved again.
Give me instead
A season in the lodge,
With a broken toe perhaps,
A tiny fracture please,
A touch of rum,
Or a passing cup,
And a stirring tale
Of the heroes
Of Telemark.

Wood Valley Temple,
Under the sugarcane moon,
Bring peace to my heart.

In Some Distant Land (for Judy)

in some distant land
i'll weave you a lei of stars
and fill your wine glass with oceans
bluer than you have guessed
my love for you will grow
like the kittens you adore
but don't tempt me to grow young
i am what i was before
and i can't unshed the tears
that fell before you kissed me
yet i'll buy you new time
with polished, ancient coins
just hold me before i kiss you
and i'll give you a love
that's newer than the white snow
that never falls for lovers
in some distant land

How to Become a Poet

there's nothing to it
buy a flannel shirt
wear it till it becomes
a petri dish
drink only the cheapest gin
for breakfast
sing ave maria
in synagogues
weep real tears
for byron
hire a naughty lady
to discuss insects
and synecdoche
sing around the campfire
with winos
fly the flag
of unacknowledged legislation
if you're a woman
curse the curse
wear tall boots
affect three names
even if you aren't
publish in shopping guides
but dream of appearing
in *the new yorker*
eschew punctuation
and napkins
blow your nose
on dollar bills
bleed your

writing heart out
and once you're done
if indeed you ever are
fly on cannabis wings
to holy trinity church
stratford-upon-avon
get down on your
altared knees
and pray to be forgiven
for what you've writ

May death come gently:
A flock of October geese
winging their way south.

As a poet and professor, Alan Howard has traversed imaginative and earthly geographies. These travels began at age six with "The Adventures of President Ub," and eventually took him to three different universities where he claims to have amassed enough knowledge to find out just how much he didn't know. As Professor of English at Bay de Noc Community College, his intimacy with the word brought a generation of Upper Peninsula students into the world of literature. Alan Howard's poems (like his life) travel to a world where both he and we newly encounter ourselves in the fine frenzy his muse inspires.